PIANO · VOCAL · GUITAR

CHRISTIAN CHART HITS

ISBN 978-1-4950-7353-3

HAL•LEONARD®

7777 W. BLUEMOUND RD. P.O. BOX 13819 MILWAUKEE, WI 53213

Visit Hal Leonard Online at
www.halleonard.com

CONTENTS

ALL THIS TIME

Words and Music by BEN GLOVER,
BRITT NICOLE and DAVID GARCIA

Moderate Pop Rock

I re-mem-ber the mo-ment, I re-mem-ber the pain. __

__ I was on-ly a girl, __ but I grew up that __ day. __

__ Tears were fall-ing; __ I know You saw me

ALL THE PEOPLE SAID AMEN

Words and Music by MATT MAHER,
PAUL MOAK and TREVOR MORGAN

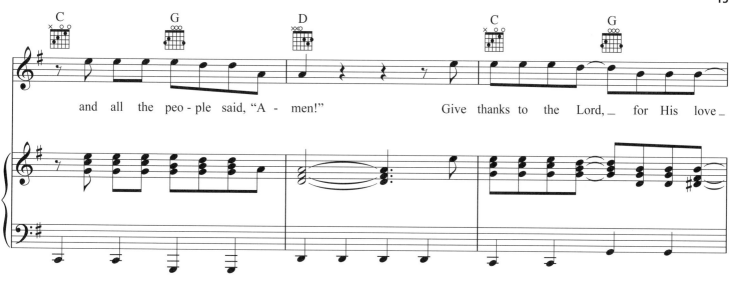

and all the peo-ple said, "A - men!"   Give thanks to the Lord, _ for His love _

_ nev - er ends. _   And all the peo - ple said, "A - men!"   Yeah! _

(band in)

men!"   And all the peo - ple said, "A - men!"

BEFORE THE MORNING

Words and Music by JOSH WILSON
and BEN GLOVER

BLESSINGS

Words and Music by
LAURA MIXON STORY

We pray ___ for bless ___ ings;
We pray ___ for wis ___ dom,

we pray ___ for peace, ___
Your voice ___ to hear. ___

com - fort ___ for fam -
And we cry ___ in an -

* Recorded a half step higher.

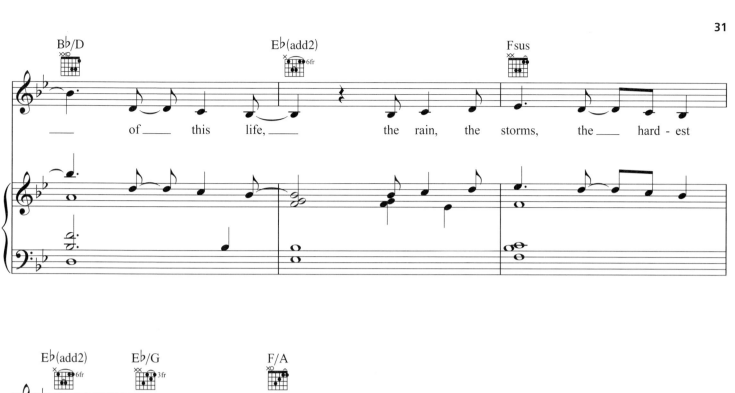

of ___ this life, ___ the rain, the storms, the ___ hard - est

nights, are Your mer - cies in ___ dis - guise? ___

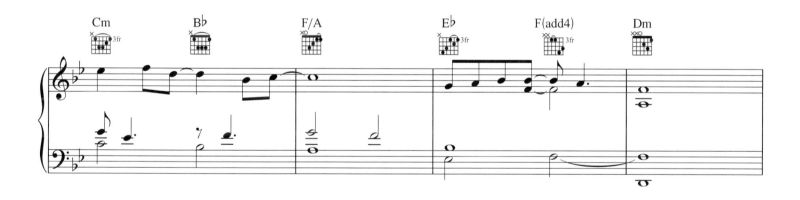

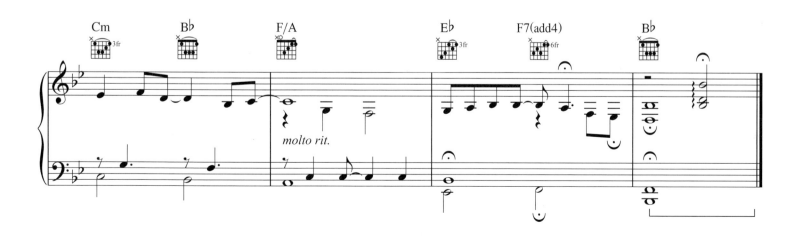

molto rit.

BROKEN TOGETHER

Words and Music by BERNIE HERMS
and MARK HALL

EVERY GOOD THING

Words and Music by BEN GLOVER,
DAVID GARCIA, JOSH HAVENS
and MATT FUQUA

Pop Rock

I _____ tend to be _____ bus - i - er than I should be, _____

There _____ will be days _____ that give me more than I can take, _____

_____ and I _____ tend to think _____ that

_____ but I know _ that You _____ al - ways make _____

* Recorded a half step higher.

To Coda

EYE OF THE STORM

Words and Music by BRYAN FOWLER
and RYAN STEVENSON

Steady Rock beat

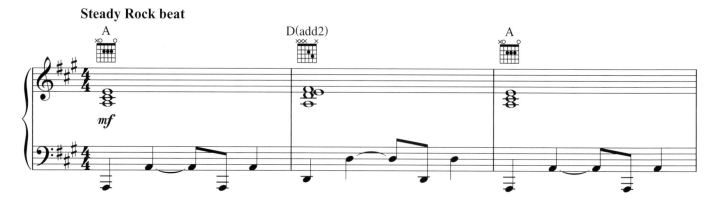

When the sol - id ground ___ is fall - ing out ___ from
hopes and dreams ___ are far from me _____ and I'm

un - der - neath ___ my feet, ___ be - tween the black skies ___ and my red ___ eyes, ___
run - ning out ___ of faith, ___ I see the fu - ture ___ I ___ pic - ture ___

DAY ONE

Words and Music by PETE KIPLEY
and MATTHEW WEST

-'ry sin-gle day Your grace re-minds __ me that my best days are not be-hind __ me. Wher-

ev-er my yes-ter-day may find __ me, well, I don't have to stay there, __ no.

See, my ho-ur-glass is up-side down __ and my "some-day soon" is here __ and now. __

__ The clock is tick-ing and I'm so sick and tired of miss-ing out. __ I

FOREVER
(We Sing Hallelujah)

Words and Music by BRIAN JOHNSON,
CHRISTA BLACK GIFFORD, GABRIEL WILSON,
JENN JOHNSON, JOEL TAYLOR and KARI JOBE

Moderately

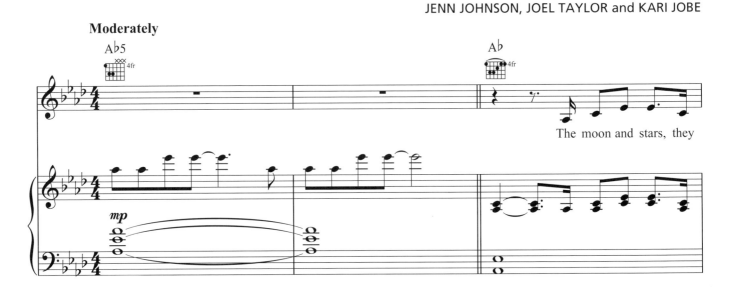

The moon and stars, they

wept; the morn-ing sun was dead. The Sav-ior of the world was fall - en.

His bod-y on ___ the cross, ___ His blood poured out for us; the weight of ev - 'ry

GIVE ME YOUR EYES

Words and Music by JASON INGRAM
and BRANDON HEATH

Recorded a half step lower.

GREATER

GREATER

Words and Music by BART MILLARD,
MIKE SCHEUCHZER, NATHAN COCHRAN,
ROBBY SHAFFER, BARRY GRAUL,
DAVID GARCIA and BEN GLOVER

Moderately fast

Ooh, ooh, ooh, ooh. Bring your

tired and bring your shame, bring your guilt and bring your
doubts and bring your fears, bring your hurt and bring your

pain. Don't you know that's not your name?
tears. There'll be no con-dem-na-tion here;

GOD IS ON THE MOVE

Words and Music by IAN ESKELIN,
CLIFF WILLIAMS, MIKEY HOWARD
and TONY WOOD

* *Recorded a half step lower.*

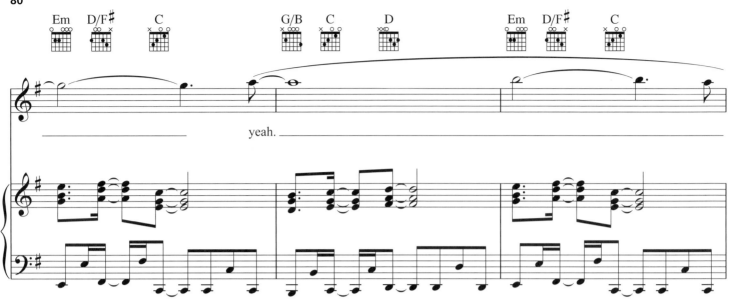

IT'S NOT OVER YET

Words and Music by BEN GLOVER,
LUKE SMALLBONE, JOEL SMALLBONE,
TEDD TJORNHOM and KYLE RICTOR

GOOD TO BE ALIVE

Words and Music by BRANDON HEATH,
JASON INGRAM and JASON GRAY

HE KNOWS

Words and Music by JEREMY CAMP
and SETH MOSLEY

I NEED A MIRACLE

Words and Music by MAC POWELL,
TAI ANDERSON, DAVID CARR
and MARK LEE

LEAD ME

Words and Music by JASON INGRAM,
MATT HAMMITT and CHRIS ROHMAN

Moderate Pop Rock

I look a-round
I see their fac - es,

and see my won-der-ful life, _____ al - most per - fect
look in their in - no - cent eyes; _____ they're just chil - dren

from the out - side. In pic - ture frames,
from the out - side. I'm work - ing hard,

* *Recorded a half step higher.*

LIVE LIKE THAT

Words and Music by BEN GLOVER,
DAVID FREY and BEN McDONALD

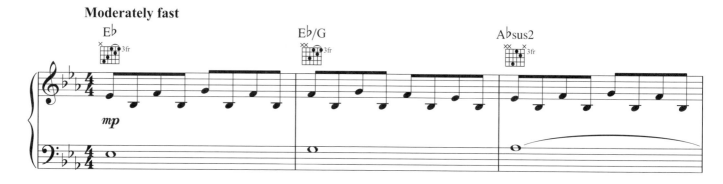

TELL YOUR HEART TO BEAT AGAIN

Words and Music by RANDY PHILLIPS,
MATTHEW WEST and BERNIE HERMS

MORE OF YOU

Words and Music by BEN GLOVER,
DAVID ARTHUR GARCIA and COLTON DIXON

THY WILL

Words and Music by BERNIE HERMS,
EMILY WEISBAND and HILLARY SCOTT

OVERCOMER

Words and Music by CHRIS STEVENS,
BEN GLOVER and DAVID GARCIA

Star-ing at a stop sign,
watch-ing peo-ple drive by, t-Mac on the ra - di - o. ___

SPEAK LIFE

Words and Music by TOBY McKEEHAN,
JAMIE MOORE and RYAN STEVENSON

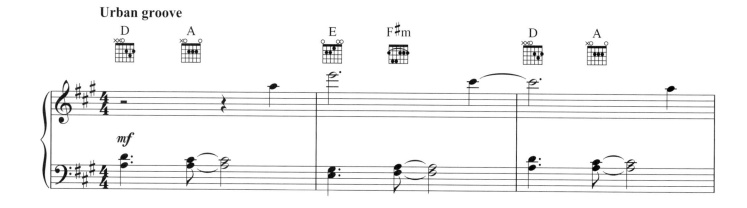

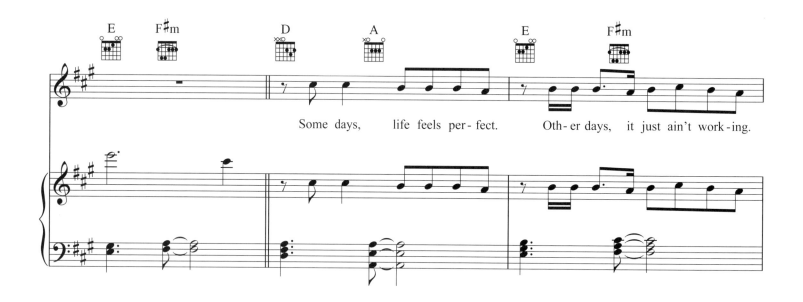

Some days, life feels per- fect. Oth- er days, it just ain't work- ing.

The good, the bad, the right, the wrong and ev -'ry- thing in be - tween.

THERE IS POWER

Words and Music by MIA FIELDES
and LINCOLN BREWSTER

TRUST IN YOU

Words and Music by MICHAEL FARREN,
LAUREN ASHLEY DAIGLE and PAUL MABURY

Moderate Pop beat

Let-ting go of ev-'ry sin-gle dream, I lay each one down

at Your feet. Ev-'ry mo-ment of my wan-der-ing

nev-er chang-es what You see. ___ I've tried to win this war,

WE BELIEVE

Words and Music by TRAVIS RYAN,
MATTHEW HOOPER and RICHIE FIKE

In this time ___ of des- per- a - tion,

when all we know ___ is doubt and ___ fear,

WHERE I BELONG

Words and Music by JASON INGRAM
and JASON ROY

Some-times it feels like I'm watch - ing from the out - side.

Some-times it feels like I'm breath - ing, but am I a - live? I won't keep search-ing for an-

- swers that aren't here to find. ____

* Recorded a half step lower.

WHOM SHALL I FEAR
(God of Angel Armies)

Words and Music by CHRIS TOMLIN,
ED CASH and SCOTT CASH

WRITE YOUR STORY

Words and Music by BEN GLOVER
and FRANCESCA BATTISTELLI

They say You're the King of ev - 'ry - thing, the One who taught the wind to sing, the source of the rhy - thm my heart keeps beat - ing. And they ____ say You can give the blind their heart

YOU ARE MORE

Words and Music by JASON INGRAM
and MIKE DONEHEY

Moderately slow Rock, in 2

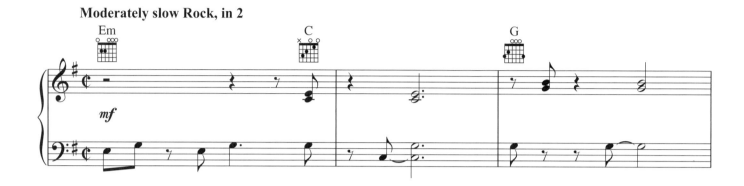

There's a girl in ___ the cor - ner

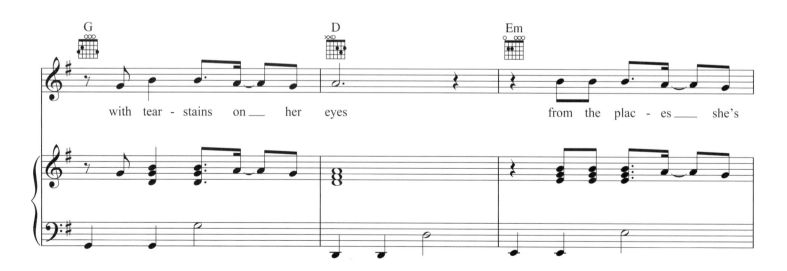

with tear - stains on ___ her eyes   from the plac - es ___ she's

Contemporary Christian Artist Folios from Hal Leonard
Arranged for Piano, Voice and Guitar

CASTING CROWNS – THRIVE
All the tracks from this popular Christian band's 2014 album, including the lead single "All You've Ever Wanted," plus: Broken Together • Dream for You • Follow Me • House of Their Dreams • Just Be Held • Thrive • and more.
00125333 P/V/G.............$16.99

THE JEREMY CAMP COLLECTION
A collection of 21 of this Dove Award-winner's best, including: Empty Me • Healing Hand of God • Jesus Saves • Let It Fade • Right Here • Stay • Take You Back • Walk by Faith • and more.
00307200 P/V/G.............$17.99

THE KIRK FRANKLIN COLLECTION
16 of Kirk Franklin's most popular gospel hits: Declaration (This Is It) • Help Me Believe • I Smile • Lean on Me • Looking for You • Jesus • Now Behold the Lamb • Stomp • Whatcha Lookin' 4? • Why We Sing • and more.
00307222 P/V/G.............$17.99

THE VERY BEST OF HILLSONG
25 songs from the popular worldwide church including: Came to My Rescue • From the Inside Out • Hosanna • I Give You My Heart • Lead Me to the Cross • Mighty to Save • Shout to the Lord • The Stand • Worthy Is the Lamb • and more.
00312101 P/V/G.............$17.99

HILLSONG MODERN WORSHIP HITS
20 songs, including: Alive • Broken Vessels (Amazing Grace) • Christ Is Enough • Cornerstone • Forever Reign • God Is Able • Mighty to Save • The Stand • This I Believe (The Creed) • Touch the Sky • and more.
00154952 P/V/G.............$16.99

HILLSONG UNITED – EMPIRES
A dozen songs from the "Empires" collection by top Christian artists who have performed at Australia's Hillsong Church: Closer Than You Know • Empires • Heart like Heaven • Here Now (Madness) • and more.
00156715 P/V/G.............$16.99

KARI JOBE – WHERE I FIND YOU
12 songs from Jobe's sophomore CD: Find You on My Knees • Here • Love Came Down • One Desire • Rise • Run to You (I Need You) • Savior's Here • Stars in the Sky • Steady My Heart • We Are • We Exalt Your Name • What Love Is This.
00307381 P/V/G.....................$16.99

THE BEST OF MERCYME
20 of the best from these Texan Christian rockers, including: All of Creation • Beautiful • Bring the Rain • God with Us • Here with Me • Homesick • The Hurt and the Healer • I Can Only Imagine • Move • Word of God Speak • and more.
00118899 P/V/G.............$17.99

MERCYME – WELCOME TO THE NEW
This 2014 album reached #1 on the Billboard® Top Christian Album charts and as high as #4 on the Billboard® 200 album charts. Our matching songbook includes all ten tracks from the CD: Burn Baby Burn • Flawless • Greater • New Lease on Life • Shake • Welcome to the New • and more.
00128518 P/V/G.....................$16.99

THE BEST OF PASSION
Over 40 worship favorites featuring the talents of David Crowder, Matt Redman, Chris Tomlin, and others. Songs include: Always • Awakening • Blessed Be Your Name • Here for You • How Marvelous • Jesus Paid It All • My Heart Is Yours • Our God • 10,000 Reasons (Bless the Lord) • You Are My King (Amazing Love) • and more.
00101888 P/V/G.....................$19.99

MATT REDMAN – SING LIKE NEVER BEFORE: THE ESSENTIAL COLLECTION
Our matching folio features 15 songs, including "10,000 Reasons (Bless the Lord)" and: Better Is One Day • The Father's Song • The Heart of Worship • Love So High • Nothing but the Blood • and more.
00116963 P/V/G.....................$16.99

SWITCHFOOT – THE BEST YET
This greatest hits compilation features the newly released song "This Is Home" and 17 other top songs. Includes: Concrete Girl • Dare You to Move • Learning to Breathe • Meant to Live • Only Hope • Stars • and more.
00307030 P/V/G $17.99

TENTH AVENUE NORTH – THE LIGHT MEETS THE DARK
The very latest from this Florida CCM band contains 11 songs, the hit single "You Are More" and: All the Pretty Things • Any Other Way • Empty My Hands • Healing Begins • House of Mirrors • Oh My Dear • On and On • Strong Enough to Save • The Truth Is Who You Are.
00307148 P/V/G.....................$16.99

THIRD DAY – LEAD US BACK: SONGS OF WORSHIP
All 12 tracks from Third Day's first collection of all-orginal worship songs: Father of Lights • He Is Alive • I Know You Can • In Jesus Name • Lead Us Back • Maker • The One I Love • Our Deliverer • Soul on Fire • Spirit • Victorious • Your Words.
00145263 P/V/G.....................$16.99

CHRIS TOMLIN – BURNING LIGHTS
A dozen songs from the 2013 release from this Christian songwriting giant! Includes the lead single "Whom Shall I Fear (God of Angel Armies)" plus: Awake My Soul • Countless Wonders • God's Great Dance Floor • Lay Me Down • Sovereign • and more.
00115644 P/V/G.....................$16.99

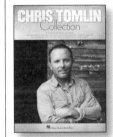

THE CHRIS TOMLIN COLLECTION – 2ND EDITION
This second edition features a fresh mix of 15 Tomlin favorites, including: Amazing Grace (My Chains Are Gone) • Forever • Holy Is the Lord • How Great Is Our God • Jesus Loves Me • Jesus Messiah • Our God • Waterfall • We Fall Down • and more.
00306951 P/V/G.....................$16.99

CHRIS TOMLIN – LOVE RAN RED
Matching piano/vocal/guitar arrangements to Tomlin's 2014 release featuring 12 tracks: Almighty • At the Cross (Love Ran Red) • Fear Not • Greater • Jesus Loves Me • The Roar • Waterfall • and more.
00139166 P/V/G.............$16.99

THE BEST OF MATTHEW WEST
16 top singles from popular Christian artist Matthew West arranged for piano, voice and guitar. Includes: Do Something • Forgiveness • Grace Wins • Mended • Only Grace • Strong Enough • When I Say I Do • You Are Everything • and more.
00159489 P/V/G.....................$16.99

For a complete listing of the products we have available, visit us online at www.halleonard.com

Prices, contents, and availability subject to change without notice.

0916

The Best
PRAISE & WORSHIP
Songbooks for Piano

Above All
THE PHILLIP KEVEREN SERIES
15 beautiful praise song piano solo arrangements by Phillip Keveren. Includes: Above All • Agnus Dei • Breathe • Draw Me Close • He Is Exalted • I Stand in Awe • Step by Step • We Fall Down • You Are My King (Amazing Love) • and more.
00311024 Piano Solo.................................$11.95

The Best Praise & Worship Songs Ever
80 all-time favorites: Awesome God • Breathe • Days of Elijah • Here I Am to Worship • I Could Sing of Your Love Forever • Open the Eyes of My Heart • Shout to the Lord • We Bow Down • dozens more.
00311057 P/V/G $22.99

More of the Best Praise & Worship Songs Ever
76 more contemporary worship favorites, including: Beautiful One • Everlasting God • Friend of God • How Great Is Our God • In Christ Alone • Let It Rise • Mighty to Save • Your Grace Is Enough • more.
00311800 P/V/G $24.99

The Big Book of Praise & Worship
Over 50 worship favorites are presented in this popular "Big Book" series collection. Includes: Always • Cornerstone • Forever Reign • I Will Follow • Jesus Paid It All • Lord, I Need You • Mighty to Save • Our God • Stronger • 10,000 Reasons (Bless the Lord) • This Is Amazing Grace • and more.
00140795 P/V/G $22.99

Contemporary Worship Duets
arr. Bill Wolaver
Contains 8 powerful songs carefully arranged by Bill Wolaver as duets for intermediate-level players: Agnus Dei • Be unto Your Name • He Is Exalted • Here I Am to Worship • I Will Rise • The Potter's Hand • Revelation Song • Your Name.
00290593 Piano Duets $10.99

51 Must-Have Modern Worship Hits
A great collection of 51 of today's most popular worship songs, including: Amazed • Better Is One Day • Everyday • Forever • God of Wonders • He Reigns • How Great Is Our God • Offering • Sing to the King • You Are Good • and more.
00311428 P/V/G $22.99

Hillsong Worship Favorites
12 powerful worship songs arranged for piano solo: At the Cross • Came to My Rescue • Desert Song • Forever Reign • Holy Spirit Rain Down • None but Jesus • The Potter's Hand • The Stand • Stronger • and more.
00312522 Piano Solo.................................$12.99

The Best of Passion
Over 40 worship favorites featuring the talents of David Crowder, Matt Redman, Chris Tomlin, and others. Songs include: Always • Awakening • Blessed Be Your Name • Jesus Paid It All • My Heart Is Yours • Our God • 10,000 Reasons (Bless the Lord) • and more.
00101888 P/V/G $19.99

Praise & Worship Duets
THE PHILLIP KEVEREN SERIES
8 worshipful duets by Phillip Keveren: As the Deer • Awesome God • Give Thanks • Great Is the Lord • Lord, I Lift Your Name on High • Shout to the Lord • There Is a Redeemer • We Fall Down.
00311203 Piano Duet $11.95

Shout to the Lord!
THE PHILLIP KEVEREN SERIES
14 favorite praise songs, including: As the Deer • El Shaddai • Give Thanks • Great Is the Lord • How Beautiful • More Precious Than Silver • Oh Lord, You're Beautiful • A Shield About Me • Shine, Jesus, Shine • Shout to the Lord • Thy Word • and more.
00310699 Piano Solo $12.95

The Chris Tomlin Collection – 2nd Edition
15 songs from one of the leading artists and composers in Contemporary Christian music, including the favorites: Amazing Grace (My Chains Are Gone) • Holy Is the Lord • How Can I Keep from Singing • How Great Is Our God • Jesus Messiah • Our God • We Fall Down • and more.
00306951 P/V/G $16.99

Top Worship Downloads
20 of today's chart-topping Christian hits, including: Cornerstone • Forever Reign • Great I Am • Here for You • Lord, I Need You • My God • Never Once • One Thing Remains (Your Love Never Fails) • Your Great Name • and more.
00120870 P/V/G $16.99

Worship Together Piano Solo Favorites
A dozen great worship songs tastefully arranged for intermediate piano solo. Includes: Amazing Grace (My Chains Are Gone) • Beautiful Savior (All My Days) • Facedown • The Heart of Worship • How Great Is Our God • and more.
00311477 Piano Solo.................................$12.95

Worship Without Words
arr. Ken Medema
The highly creative Ken Medema has arranged 13 worship songs and classic hymns, perfect for blended worship. Includes: As the Deer • I Could Sing of Your Love Forever • Open the Eyes of My Heart • You Are My All in All • and more.
00311229 Piano Solo.................................$12.95

THE BEST SACRED COLLECTIONS FOR PIANO

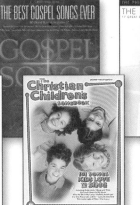

The Big Book of Hymns

An invaluable collection of 125 favorite hymns, including: All Hail the Power of Jesus' Name • Battle Hymn of the Republic • Blessed Assurance • For the Beauty of the Earth • Holy, Holy, Holy • It Is Well with My Soul • Just as I Am • A Mighty Fortress Is Our God • The Old Rugged Cross • Onward Christian Soldiers • Rock of Ages • Sweet By and By • What a Friend We Have in Jesus • Wondrous Love • and more.
00310510 P/V/G $17.95

The Best Gospel Songs Ever

80 of the best-loved gospel songs of all time: Amazing Grace • At Calvary • Because He Lives • Behold the Lamb • Daddy Sang Bass • His Eye Is on the Sparrow • His Name Is Wonderful • How Great Thou Art • I Saw the Light • I'll Fly Away • Just a Closer Walk with Thee • Just a Little Talk with Jesus • Mansion over the Hilltop • The Old Rugged Cross • Peace in the Valley • Will the Circle Be Unbroken • Wings of a Dove • more.
00310503 P/V/G $19.99

Hymns for Easy Classical Piano

arr. Phillip Keveren

15 beloved songs of faith masterfully presented in a classical style for easy piano. Includes: Abide with Me • A Mighty Fortress Is Our God • Praise God, from Whom All Blessings Flow • in Jesus • Were You There? • and more.
00160294 Easy Piano $12.99

The Christian Children's Songbook

101 songs from Sunday School, all in appropriate keys for children's voices. Includes: Awesome God • The B-I-B-L-E • Clap Your Hands • Day by Day • He's Got the Whole World in His Hands • Jesus Loves Me • Let There Be Peace on Earth • This Little Light of Mine • more.
00310472 P/V/G $19.95

The Hymn Collection

arranged by Phillip Keveren

17 beloved hymns expertly and beautifully arranged for solo piano by Phillip Keveren. Includes: All Hail the Power of Jesus' Name • I Love to Tell the Story • I Surrender All • I've Got Peace Like a River • Were You There? • and more.
00311071 Piano Solo $12.99

P/V/G = Piano/Vocal/Guitar arrangements.
Prices, contents and availability subject to change without notice.

Hymn Duets

arranged by Phillip Keveren

Includes lovely duet arrangements of: All Creatures of Our God and King • I Surrender All • It Is Well with My Soul • O Sacred Head, Now Wounded • Praise to the Lord, The Almighty • Rejoice, The Lord Is King • and more.
00311544 Piano Duet $10.95

Hymn Medleys

arranged by Phillip Keveren

Great medleys resonate with the human spirit, as do the truths in these moving hymns. Here Phillip Keveren combines 24 timeless favorites into eight lovely medleys for solo piano.
00311349 Piano Solo $12.99

Hymns for Two

arranged by Carol Klose

12 piano duet arrangements of favorite hymns: Amazing Grace • Be Thou My Vision • Crown Him with Many Crowns • Fairest Lord Jesus • Holy, Holy, Holy • I Need Thee Every Hour • O Worship the King • What a Friend We Have in Jesus • and more.
00290544 Piano Duet $10.99

Ragtime Gospel Hymns

arranged by Steven Tedesco

15 traditional gospel hymns, including: At Calvary • Footsteps of Jesus • Just a Closer Walk with Thee • Leaning on the Everlasting Arms • What a Friend We Have in Jesus • When We All Get to Heaven • and more.
00311763 Piano Solo $8.95

Seasonal Sunday Solos for Piano

24 blended selections grouped by occasion. Includes: Breath of Heaven (Mary's Song) • Come, Ye Thankful People, Come • Do You Hear What I Hear • God of Our Fathers • In the Name of the Lord • Mary, Did You Know? • Mighty to Save • Spirit of the Living God • The Wonderful Cross • and more.
00311971 Piano Solo $14.99

Sunday Solos for Piano

30 blended selections, perfect for the church pianist. Songs include: All Hail the Power of Jesus' Name • Be Thou My Vision • Great Is the Lord • Here I Am to Worship • Majesty • Open the Eyes of My Heart • and many more.
00311272 Piano Solo $16.99

More Sunday Solos for Piano

A follow-up to *Sunday Solos for Piano*, this collection features 30 more blended selections perfect for the church pianist. Includes: Agnus Dei • Come, Thou Fount of Every Blessing • The Heart of Worship • How Great Thou Art • Immortal, Invisible • O Worship the King • Shout to the Lord • Thy Word • We Fall Down • and more.
00311864 Piano Solo $15.99

Even More Sunday Solos for Piano

30 blended selections, including: Ancient Words • Brethren, We Have Met to Worship • How Great Is Our God • Lead On, O King Eternal • Offering • Savior, Like a Shepherd Lead Us • We Bow Down • Worthy of Worship • and more.
00312098 Piano Solo $14.99

Weekly Worship
52 HYMNS FOR A YEAR OF PRAISE

arr. Phillip Keveren

52 hymns that will keep you playing all year long! Each song also includes a brief history by Lindsay Rickard. Hymns include: Abide with Me • All Creatures of Our God and King • Amazing Grace • Be Thou My Vision • It Is Well with My Soul • Just As I Am • The Old Rugged Cross • Savior, like a Shepherd Lead Us • When I Survey the Wondrous Cross • and more.
00145342 Easy Piano.......................... $16.99

HAL•LEONARD®

www.halleonard.com

0916